Learn to Quilt

Row by Row™

by **LINDA CAUSEE**

Table of Contents

At the Seashore

Approximate Size: 59½" x 70"

Techniques
Sky Row: Machine Appliqué (page 15)
Sailboat Row: Half-Square Triangles (page 7)
Water Rows: Seminole Piecing (page 6)
Fish Row: Stitch and Flip (page 8)
Beach Rows: Foundation Piecing (page 9)

Materials
1½ yds lt blue sky fabric (sky)
⅝ yd white (birds, clouds)
fat quarter yellow (sun)
⅛ yd red (sailboat)
⅛ yd green (sailboat)
½ yd lt turquoise (water)
1⅝ yds med turquoise (water)
½ yd dk turquoise (water)
⅜ yd orange (fish)
¼ yd gold (starfish)
Assorted peach scraps (seashells)
½ yd lt tan (sand)
⅝ yd border 1 fabric
1 yd border 2 fabric
⅝ yd binding
3¾ yds backing
Batting

Cutting Requirements
Sky Row
Note: For sun, clouds and birds, trace pattern number of times indicated below onto paper-backed fusible web. (See Machine Appliqué, page 15.)
Two 15½" x 21½" rectangles, sky fabric
One 18" x 21½" rectangle, sky fabric
One sun (pattern on page 31)
Four clouds (pattern on page 29)
Three birds (pattern on page 30)

Sailboat Row
Sailboat Blocks
16 (3") squares, sky fabric
12 (3½") squares, sky fabric
Eight 3½" squares, red
Eight 3" squares, green
Four 3½" squares, green
Eight 3½" squares, lt turquoise

Eight 3½" squares, med turquoise

Sashing
Three 3" x 8" strips, sky fabric
Two 3½" squares, lt turquoise
Two 3½" squares, med turquoise

Water Rows
Bottom Row
Two 2½"-wide strips, tan
Four 1⅜"-wide strips, dk turquoise
Two 2½"-wide strips, med turquoise
Four 1⅜"-wide strips, lt turquoise
Two 2¾"-wide strips, med turquoise

Top Row
Two 1⅜"-wide strips, dk turquoise
Two 2"-wide strips, dk turquoise
Two 2"-wide strips, med turquoise
Two 2¼"-wide strips, med turquoise
Four 1⅜"-wide strips, lt turquoise

Fish Row
Four 4" x 7½" rectangles A, orange
Four 2" x 3½" rectangles C, orange
13 (2¼" x 4") rectangles E, orange
13 (1¼" x 2") rectangles G, orange
Eight 4" squares B, med turquoise
Eight 2" squares D, med turquoise
26 (2¾") squares F, med turquoise
26 (1¾") squares H, med turquoise
Eight 2" x 2½" rectangles I, med turquoise
26 (1¼" x 1½") rectangles J, med turquoise
10 (3" x 2¼") rectangles K, med turquoise
Two 3½" x 7½" rectangles L, med turquoise (trim to fit later)

Beach Row
Note: Special cutting is not required for foundation piecing.
Additional Pieces
Three 4" squares, sand color
Four 4" x 7½" rectangles, sand color
Seven 3" x 7½" rectangles, sand color
One 4½" x 7½" rectangles, sand color

Finishing
Seven 2½"-wide border 1 strips
Seven 4½-wide border 2 strips
Seven 2½"-wide binding strips

Instructions

Sky Row—Machine Appliqué (page 15)

1. Referring to instructions for machine appliqué, page 15, trace patterns onto paper side of fusible web. Cut along drawn line.

2. Place fusible web, bumpy side down on wrong side of fabric. Iron fusible web to fabric, following manufacturer's directions. Remove paper backing from fabric shapes.

3. Referring to layout for placement, position sun and two clouds, onto right side of 15½" x 21½" blue sky rectangle and two birds on remaining 15½" x 21½" rectangle. Position two clouds and one bird on 18" x 21½" blue sky rectangle. Iron in place following manufacturer's directions.

4. Using invisible thread, machine zigzag appliqué pieces in place.

5. Sew sections together to complete row.

Sailboat Row—Half-Square Triangles (page 7)

1. Cut all 3½" squares in half diagonally.

2. Place blue sky triangle right side together with a red triangle; stitch along diagonal edge, **Fig. 1**.

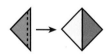

Fig. 1

3. Chain piece remaining pairs of triangles. You will need: 16 squares with blue sky and red fabrics, eight squares with blue sky and green, and 19 squares with lt and med turquoise fabrics, **Fig. 2**.

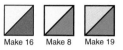

Make 16   Make 8   Make 19

Fig. 2

Hint: Place triangles in pairs with right sides together first so they will be ready for chain piecing.

4. Referring to **Fig. 3**, place squares and triangle squares in four rows of four. Sew together in rows, and then sew rows together. Repeat for remaining three blocks.

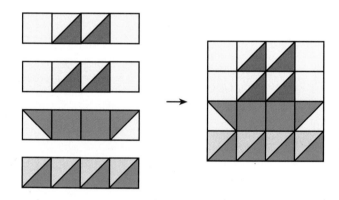

Fig. 3

5. Sew lt/med turquoise square to end of 3" x 8" strip, **Fig 4**, for sashing strip.

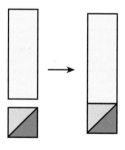

Fig. 4

6. Referring to photo, sew Sailboat blocks and sashing strips together to complete row.

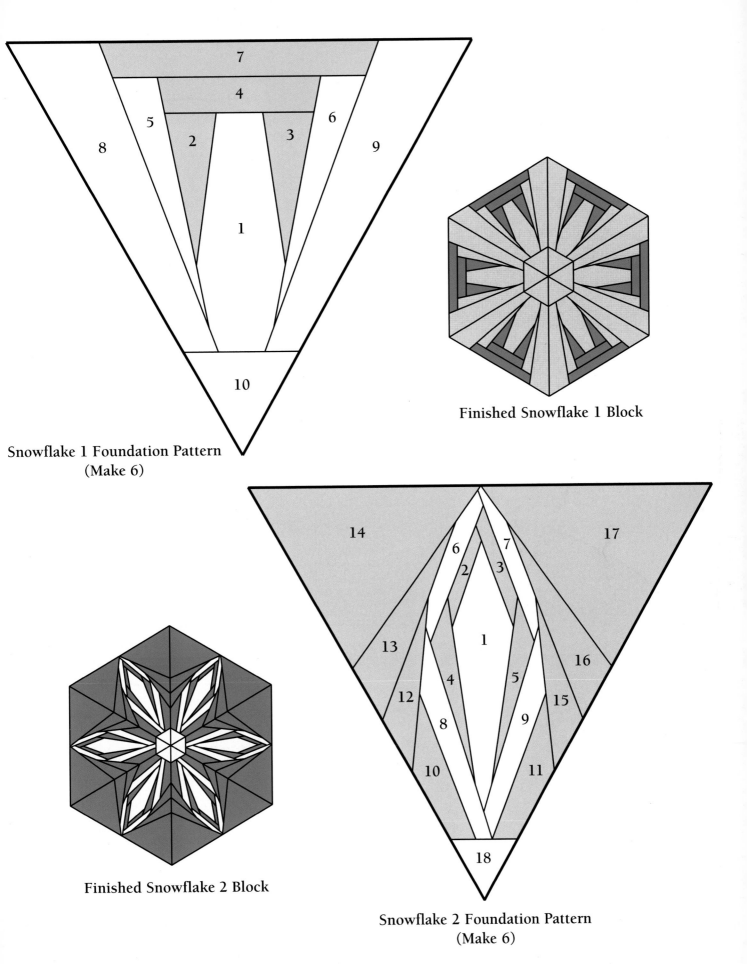

Snowflake 1 Foundation Pattern
(Make 6)

Finished Snowflake 1 Block

Finished Snowflake 2 Block

Snowflake 2 Foundation Pattern
(Make 6)

Finished Block

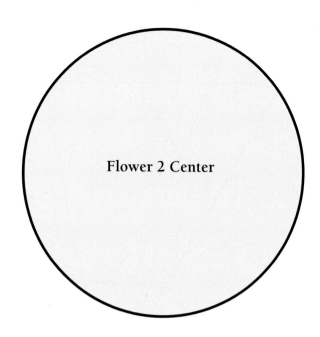

Flower 2 Center

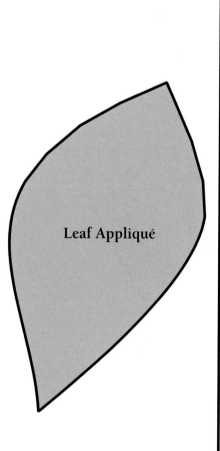

Leaf Appliqué

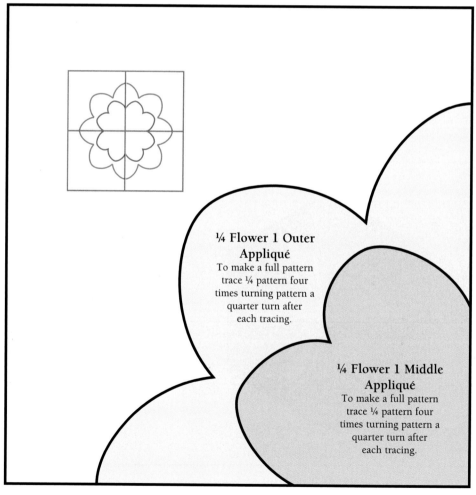

¼ Flower 1 Outer Appliqué
To make a full pattern trace ¼ pattern four times turning pattern a quarter turn after each tracing.

¼ Flower 1 Middle Appliqué
To make a full pattern trace ¼ pattern four times turning pattern a quarter turn after each tracing.

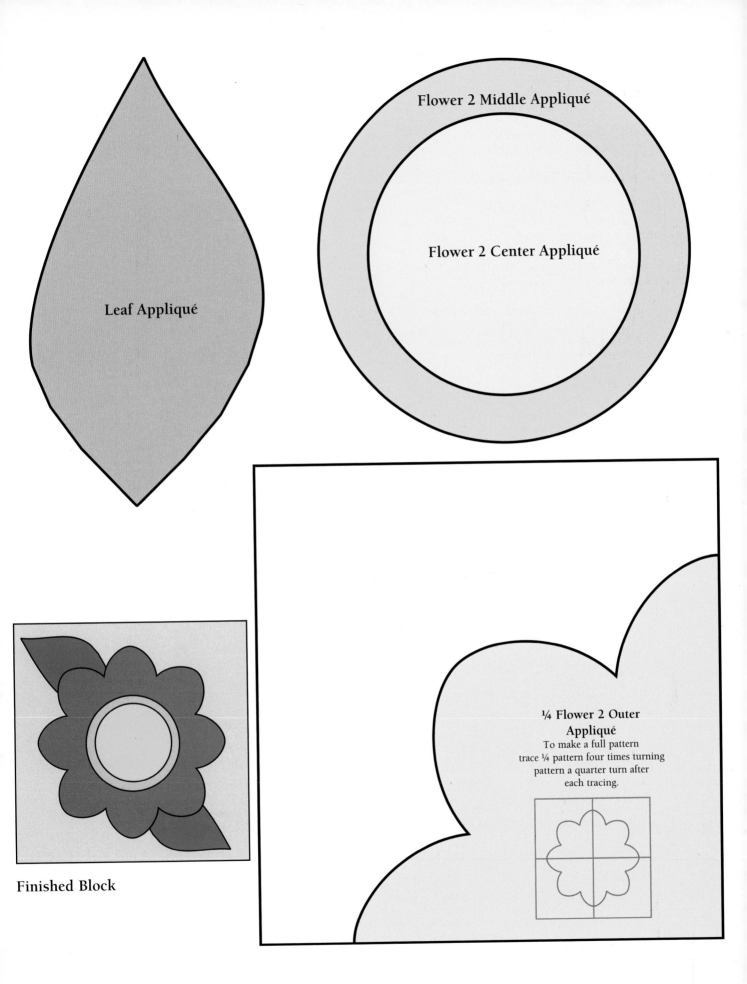

Leaf Appliqué

Flower 2 Middle Appliqué

Flower 2 Center Appliqué

Finished Block

¼ Flower 2 Outer
Appliqué
To make a full pattern
trace ¼ pattern four times turning
pattern a quarter turn after
each tracing.

Editorial: Bobbie Matela, Linda Causee, Christina Wilson
Technical Artist: Chad Summers
Production: Amy S. Lin

Thank you to the following companies who
generously supplied products for our quilts:

Bernina® of America: Artista 180 sewing machine

Güterman: 100 percent cotton sewing thread

Springs Industries, Benartex: Fabrics

Stearns Technical Textile Company: Mountain Mist®
Cream Rose 100 percent Cotton Batting

Quilts were made by: Jackie Breitenfeld, Linda Causee,
Sandy Hunter, Claire Jungerson, Heidi Nick, Robin
Radovich, Sue Ragan, Michiko Rice, Christina Wilson
Quilts machine quilted by: Faith Horsky

1455 Linda Vista Drive
San Marcos, CA 92069
www.ASNpub.com
©2003 American School of Needlework Inc.

The full line of ASN products is carried by Annie's Attic catalog.
TOLL-FREE ORDER LINE or to request a free catalog (800) 582-6643
visit www.AnniesAttic.com
Customer Service (800) 282-6643, **Fax** (800) 882-6643